Howard B. Wigglebottom
and the Power of Giving: A Christmas Story

Howard Binkow

Susan F. Cornelison

SCHOLASTIC INC.
New York Toronto London Auckland
Sydney Mexico City New Delhi Hong Kong

Howard Binkow
Rev. Ana Rowe
Susan F. Cornelison
Tobi S. Cunningham

This book is the result of a joint creative effort with Ana Rowe and Susan F. Cornelison.

Gratitude and appreciation are given to all those who reviewed the story prior to publication.
The book became much better by incorporating several of their suggestions:

Karen Binkow, Erin Gaffny, Sherry Holland, Trish Jones, Renee Keeler, Lori Kotarba, Sarah Langner, Tracy Mastalski, Teri Poulus, Laurie Sachs, Mimi C. Savio, Karey Scholten, Anne Shacklett, C.J. Shuffler, Nancey Silvers, Gayle Smith, Carrie Sutton, Rosemary Underwood, and George Sachs Walor.

Teachers, librarians, counselors, and students at:
Blackbird Elementary, Harbor Springs, Michigan
Bossier Parish Schools, Bossier City, Louisiana
Central Elementary, Beaver Falls, Pennsylvania
Chalker Elementary, Kennesaw, Georgia
Charleston Elementary, Charleston, Arkansas
Forest Avenue Elementary, Hudson, Massachusetts
Glen Alpine Elementary, Morganton, North Carolina

Golden West Elementary, Manteca, California
Iveland Elementary School, St. Louis, Missouri
Kincaid Elementary, Marietta, Georgia
Lamarque Elementary School, North Port, Florida
Lee Elementary, Los Alamitos, California
Prestonwood Elementary, Dallas, Texas
Sherman Oaks Elementary, Sherman Oaks, California
West Navarre Primary, Navarre, Florida

Merry Christmas, 2011!
Love, Mrs. Horn

This book belongs to
Ines ♡

It was Christmas time, the season for GIVING–but for Howard B. Wigglebottom, it was the season for GETTING!

Getting new things made Howard happy for a while. But soon he would get bored and want more stuff.

"Howard, you need to learn to share," said his mom. But Howard wasn't listening.

MIIIIIIINE!

"Mom, I'm almost finished with my list for Santa." "Oh, Howard," sighed his mom. "You already have way more than you need." But Howard wasn't paying attention. He was listening to TV commercials for ideas to add to his list.

"Howard, we will be going to visit your cousins tomorrow," said his mom. "Pack lots of warm clothes." But Howard wasn't listening. He packed his toys instead.

Howard and his family arrived at the station just in time. As he was getting on the train, his big bag got caught in the door and the toys spilled all over. When he hopped off to get them, the doors closed and the train left.

Howard was all alone.

Unsure where to go, he started walking. It was really cold. Howard had no money, no food and no phone. His toys were really heavy but there was no way he was leaving them there. He heard noises around him. Howard knew he wasn't alone.

KERPLOP!

He started to run but the noises followed him.

He found a place to hide. As he stood there cold and alone, he saw a family having dinner. It made him really hungry.

Howard began to cry and tears froze on his cheeks. He thought, "I wish I could be warm and home with my family. Will I ever see them again?" He sat down outside the window and soon fell sound asleep.

When Howard woke up, he heard a tiny voice saying, "Are you the Santa Bunny? I have a letter for you."

He jumped up and grabbed his things, yelling, "Leave me alone!" He was about to run, but . . .

. . . he tripped and rolled all the way down a hill. Stuck and unable to move, he watched his toys being grabbed. He tried to scream but couldn't because his mouth was full of snow.

Howard became a giant snowman.

"We just want to help Santa Bunny," said the birds as they put the toys back in the bag. "We love you."

Howard felt sad and ashamed. They weren't after his toys. Homeless like him, they were just trying to help. The blue bird gave Howard a piece of paper.

"Dear Santa Bunny," it read. "I will be so grateful if I can belong to a loving family. Thank you."

Howard felt sad and ashamed again. He had a very loving family he took for granted. He asked the others for their wishes. "A warm bed, food and someone to say 'I love you,'" they all answered.

Right then he decided to help and take them all home. He made a wish himself: "Dear Santa, please forget my other list. What I really want is to appreciate the good things I already have. Please help me."

Singing Christmas carols under the stars, they flew together
until they found the way to Howard's house.

Howard was happy to get back home. After feeding his friends and tucking them into bed, he stayed up a little longer to look at his favorite toys. He had too much stuff. Howard picked a special toy for each of his new friends. He couldn't wait to see their faces as they opened the presents. He had never felt this joy before, the joy of giving from the heart.

"If I could only have my family back again." Howard wished he could tell them he was so sorry for his old, selfish ways.

Just then the door opened and there they were!
"Howard, we've been looking all over for
you!" said his mom. "How did you find
your way home, you smart little boy?"
"My new friends helped me," Howard
said and told his family everything
that had happened. "Can they stay
over for the holidays?"

"Of course! We would love to
have them," his parents
said.

The next evening at Christmas dinner, Howard learned his parents were working on finding a home for each one of his new friends.

"MIIIIIIIINE!" shouted Howard suddenly. Everyone stopped and stared.

"Just kidding," he said. "I'm into giving and sharing now.

Happy holidays and merry Christmas, everyone!"

Howard B. Wigglebottom and the Power of Giving: A Christmas Story
Lessons and Reflections

★THE HAPPINESS OF GETTING

The first moments after we get a new toy or game, or phone or bike, we become very excited and happy. We can't part with it. It's all we can think about! But not long after, we notice that the thing doesn't bring us as much joy as before.

Where did the excitement go? How come the happiness didn't last? Well, it is because long-lasting happiness never comes from things. Howard had a room full of toys and things but he always wanted more. He couldn't stay happy for long.

Most people want to be as happy and excited as they can be for as long as possible. Like Howard in the beginning of the book, many people believe happiness comes from getting new things all the time.

How can we make happiness last for a long time? By looking for happiness in places other than toys and things.

★THE HAPPINESS OF GIVING

Howard learned that there is joy and happiness from giving. He understood he didn't need all the stuff he had and that he could make other people happy by sharing his things.

Giving brings us happiness that will last and stay with us for a long time. What else can we do to bring happiness into our lives? Here are a few examples:

- Being kind to others
- Being friendly to the kids who don't have friends
- Learning to share our things and toys
- Being grateful for what we have
- Helping people in any way we can

Can you think of something else that will bring us real and long-lasting happiness?

★LEARNING TO SHARE

Do you like to share your things and toys? Howard didn't like to share. He grabbed his toys away from his brothers and sisters. He was angry and unhappy all the time until he learned there was joy in letting other kids play with all the things he owned.

It might not be easy in the beginning. It will take practice and a little time for you to get used to and comfortable with the idea of sharing. Just like learning a new sport or a musical instrument, the more we practice the better we get. Start with a toy or a thing that you don't care about very much. When you are comfortable sharing that, then try sharing something that you really like.

★ PAYING ATTENTION TO STAY OUT OF TROUBLE

Why was Howard left all alone at the train station? Because he didn't listen to his mom! Instead of bringing a couple of sweaters for the train ride, he brought a big bag of toys that got caught in the train's door.

Most of us don't like to follow rules or to be told what to do. Then we get in trouble and don't know why! When grown-ups tell us to do something it is for our protection and because they care about us. It is not because they want us to be unhappy. So when you feel like disobeying and not paying attention, think again! You don't want bad things to happen to you. You don't want to invite unhappiness in your life!

★ HOMELESS

When Howard was left behind and the train left, he didn't know what to do. He had no phone and didn't know the way back home. He became homeless for the day–that means he had no place to sleep, eat, shower, etc. He didn't appreciate all the good things he had until he lost them all. Some people are homeless for a long, long time, until they find someone to help them.

Are you grateful for having a place to sleep, something to eat, shoes on your feet and clothes to wear? Many kids don't have any of that. Many kids don't have anyone who loves them or protects them from danger, either. What would you do if you were left behind and got lost? Did Howard do the right thing by walking away from the train station?

★ TALKING TO STRANGERS

Is it safe to talk to strangers? Was Howard scared of the strangers that were following him?

Not really. He was upset because he thought the strangers wanted his things.

What would you tell Howard if you were his mom or dad? He was lucky that the strangers were nice little birds that wanted to help. Some strangers can be nice but some can be very mean. So it is best to talk to strangers only if your teacher or an adult you know is next to you.

★ THE SPIRIT OF HOLIDAYS OR CHRISTMAS

Most of us have some kind of holiday, a special day when we are supposed to be extra nice and caring towards each other. Everybody feels good and happy. People are kind and smile a lot. When grown-ups talk about the "spirit of the holidays" they mean "Let's get happy by being nice, generous and polite with everyone."